# Memories

# Where wer you born and when?

_____

_____

_____

_____

_____

_____

_____

_____

_____

Did you have a nickname that your siblings or friends call you? How did you get the nickname?

_____

_____

_____


What were your favorite toys and what were they like?

_____

_____

_____

_____

_____

# What are the earliest memories you have?

_____

_____

_____

_____

_____

_____

_____

_____

_____

Did you get an allowance? How much was it and what did you spend your money on?

_____

_____

_____

_____

_____

_____

_____

_____

_____

_____

Did you ever get in trouble as a child or teenager? Did you have a curfew and what time was it? Did you ever miss curfew?

_____

_____

_____

_____

_____

What is different about growing up today than when you were a child?

_____

_____

_____

_____

_____

Where was the first place you lived away from home? Do you have any crazy roommate stories?

_____

_____

_____

_____

_____

_____

_____

_____

_____

_____

_____

What do/did you love most about your own dad and Mom?

_____

_____

_____

What is the best Christmas or birthday gift you've ever received and given?

_____

_____

_____

What was your favorite thing to do on the weekends?

_____

_____

_____

Did you ever have a low point as a teenager? How did you get through it?

_____

_____

_____

_____

_____

_____

_____

_____

_____

_____

Tell me about a leader who impacted your life for good when you were a kid.

_____

_____

_____

_____

Who were your friends from school and what did you do together for fun?

_____

_____

_____

_____

_____

What was the first car you drove?

_____

_____

_____

What do you appreciate most
about your parents?

_____

_____

_____

What do you appreciate most
about your parents?

_____

_____

_____

What is the most surprising thing you enjoy about being a child?

_____

_____

_____

_____

Tell me about your favorite family holiday traditions.

_____

_____

_____

_____

_____

_____

Did you do any sports or clubs when you were a teen? If so, what are your favorite memories?

_____

_____

_____

_____

_____

_____

_____

_____

_____

_____

Did you ever get really sick or have to go to the hospital?
What happened?

_____

_____

_____

_____

_____


What was the first concert you went to? How much did it cost?

_____

_____

_____

_____

_____

_____

# What are your top five best memories?

_____

_____

_____

_____

_____

_____

_____

_____

_____

_____

_____

_____

# What lessons would you like me to learn from your experiences growing up?

_____

_____

_____

_____

_____

_____

_____

_____

_____

_____

What or who was your favorite:

Animal?

_____

Athlete?

_____

Author?

_____

Board game?

_____

Book?

_____

Candy?

_____

Card game?

_____

# What or who was your favorite:

Meal?

_____

Movie star?

_____

Movie?

_____

Musical group?

_____

Musical instrument?

_____

Painting?

_____

Poem?

_____

What or who was your favorite:

Color?

_____

Cookie?

_____

Drink?

_____

Flavor of ice cream?

_____

Flower?

_____

Fruit?

_____

Holiday?

_____

What or who was your favorite:

Poet?

_____

Restaurant?

_____

Season?

_____

Singer?

_____

Song?

_____

Sport?

_____

Style of music?

_____

If you had to pick a label for your family members ( mother, father, brothers, sisters,...), who fits each of the following descriptions during your childhood?

Best cook

_____

Best gardener

_____

Best housekeeper

_____

Best looking

_____

Best memory

_____

If you had to pick a label for your family members ( mother, father, brothers, sisters,...), who fits each of the following descriptions during your childhood?

Best story teller

_____

Biggest tease

_____

Calmest

_____

Funniest

_____

Hardest worker

_____

If you had to pick a label for your family members ( mother, father, brothers, sisters,...), who fits each of the following descriptions during your childhood?

Most athletic

_____

Biggest tease

_____

Most colorful

_____

Most creative

_____

Most frugal

_____

If you had to pick a label for your family members ( mother, father, brothers, sisters,...), who fits each of the following descriptions during your childhood?

Most generous

_____

Most mischievous

_____

Most politically active

_____

Most reclusive

_____

Most relaxed

_____

If you had to pick a label for your family members ( mother, father, brothers, sisters,...), who fits each of the following descriptions during your childhood?

Most sociable

_____

Quietest

_____

Shortest

_____

Tallest

_____

Did you ever hear any stories about anything interesting that happened during or soon after your birth?

_____

_____

_____

_____

Was anything memorable and perhaps funny) said by someone during or soon after your birth? How many siblingsdid you have?

_____

_____

_____

_____

What is something that you were just never able to understand,as a child?

_____

_____

What is the funniest thing you ever remember saying, as a small child?

_____

_____

_____

Did you ever do anything really foolish, as a child?

_____

_____

_____

_____

_____

Did you ever have to sleep in the same bed as a sibling?

_____

_____

If so, which sibling in particular?

_____

_____

If you slept in the same bed with a sibling, how did you feel about having to do so?

_____

_____

_____

_____

If you had one or more older siblings, how did you get along with them?

_____

_____

_____

If you had one or more younger siblings, how did you get along with them?

_____

_____

_____

Which sibling were you the closest with?

_____

Which sibling did you quarrel the most with?

_____

_____

How would you quarrel with your sibling(s)?

_____

_____

_____

_____

How often did you spend time with your cousins?

_____

_____

_____

Who were your favorite cousins
to spend time with?

_____

_____

Where was your first childhood
home?

_____

_____

Did your first childhood home
have electricity?

_____

Did your first childhood home
have a telephone?

_____

Whom did your parents talk to on the phone most often?

_____

_____

What did your childhood house look like?

_____

_____

How big or small was your childhood home?

_____

_____

What rooms were there in your childhoodhome?

_____

_____

_____

Do you remember any particular smells or scents from your childhood home?

_____

_____

Can you recall any familiar sounds or noises from your childhood home?

_____

_____

What kinds of sounds and smells do you remember when you first woke up in the morning?

_____

Did everyone in your household speak English as their first language?

_____

_____

Were you or anyone in your family able to speak a language other than English?

_____

_____

If so, when and how did they learn that language?

_____

_____

What were your pets' names?

_____

_____

How and when did your family get those pets?

_____

_____

_____

Who got to choose those pets' names, and how were they decided?

_____

_____

_____

Did you have to work to convince your parents to get the pet? If so, how did you finally convince them?

_____

_____

_____

_____

Did the pet(s) belong to you personally or did the pet(s) belong to one of your siblings, or did the pet(s) belong to the whole family?

_____

_____

_____

Who cared for the pet(s) (fed them, cleaned up after them, took them for walks, etc.)?

_____

_____

What was involved in caring for your pet(s)?

_____

_____

What kinds of games or activities did you play with your pet(s)?

_____

_____

How long did the pet(s) live?

_____

_____

How did you feel when each pet died?

_____

_____

How would you usually cool off during
the summer, when you were a child?

_____

_____

How would you usually warm up during
the winter, when you were a child?

_____

_____

What was your favorite meal,
growing up?

_____

Who cooked that meal the best?

_____

_____

What was your least favorite food,
growing up?

_____

_____

What would your parents say or do if
you didn't finish some of your food?

_____

_____

What were family meals like,
in your household?

_____

_____

_____

Did you all sit and eat together for every meal?

_____

_____

What kinds of topics were discussed at the family dinner table?

_____

_____

_____

_____

Were there any topics that were off-limits at the family dinner table? If so, which topics?

_____

_____

_____

_____

Did your family ever grow, pickle, can, or home-make any food?

_____

_____

_____

_____

What kind of oven did you have in your kitchen, when you were a child?

_____

_____

Did you ever cook or help with the cooking, as a child?

_____

_____

_____

Did your household ever have a cooking disaster, or a meal that turned out really badly one time? If so, were you responsible for it?

_____

_____

_____

What kind of refrigerator did you have in your kitchen, when you were a child?

_____

_____

What would your parents do for you when you were sick? Any special remedies?

_____

_____

_____

_____

What was the sickest you ever got, as a child?

_____

_____

_____

Who was your best friend, as a child?

_____

_____

How did you and your best friend become friends?

_____

_____

_____

_____

What kind of games did you play as a child?

_____

_____

_____

What was your favorite game to play?

_____

Did you ever play any video games, or carnival games as a child?
If so, which ones?

_____

_____

Which video, arcade, or carnival game were you the best at?

_____

_____

What was your favorite toy to play with?

_____

How big was your yard?

_____

_____

_____

What kind of trees or flowers grew on your property?

_____

_____

_____

What kind of critters (bugs, birds, small animals, etc.) would you find on your property?

_____

_____

_____

Did you ever catch any bugs or animals on your property and try to keep them as a pet?

_____

_____

_____

Did you ever have your own garden as a child, or did you ever help someone else out with their garden?

_____

_____

_____

Did you live in the city or on a farm?

_____

If you lived on a farm, what kind of produce and livestock did your family raise?

_____

_____

_____

If you lived on a farm, what kind of farm-related chores were you responsible for?

_____

_____

What was your favorite farm-related chore to do?

_____

What was your least favorite farm-related choreto do?

_____

If you lived on a farm, did you ever give names to any of the farm animals?

_____

_____

_____

If your family farmed or made produce, did you sell it at a grocery store or a farmer's market perhaps?

_____

_____

If so, which market, and where was it located?

_____

_____

Did you have a favorite treat you liked to buy for yourself at the grocery store or the soda shop?

_____

_____

What was it, and how much did it cost you?

_____

_____

Did you have a piano or a pump organ in your house, as a child?

_____

_____

Did you ever take piano lessons or try to teach yourself to play the piano?

_____

_____

If so, how good at playing the piano were you?

_____

Who were your family's next door neighbors when you were a child?

_____

_____

_____

What were your next door neighbors like? Friendly, mean, sociable, reclusive, etc.?

_____

_____

_____

_____

_____

_____

How old were your next door neighbors?

_____

How often did your family or your next door neighbors visit with each other?

_____

_____

_____

Did you ever receive any gifts from your neighbors?

_____

If so, what were they?

_____

_____

_____

Who would baby sit you when your parents weren't home?

_____

Who was your favorite baby sitter?

_____

What kind of games or activities would your babysitter do with you?

_____

_____

_____

Who cut your hair, when you were
a child?

_____

_____

what was your usual style of haircut,
when you were little?

_____

_____

Did you ever cut your own hair?

_____

If so, how did that turn out?

_____

_____

How often would your parents take you to get new shoes?

_____

_____

Do you remember where your family bought shoes?

_____

_____

How would you dress, as a child?

_____

_____

_____

_____

_____

Did your family ever home-make any clothing?

_____

_____

If so, who made the clothing In your family?

_____

_____

If your family home-made clothing, how did they do it?

_____

_____

_____

_____

If your family clothing, what materials did they use?

_____

_____

_____

If your family bought clothing from a store, which store(s) did your family buy clothing from?

_____

_____

_____

_____

On what occasions would you get new clothing or new outfits?

_____

_____

_____

Do you remember any words or sayings that were common in your youth that nobody says anymore?

_____

_____

_____

Did you have a bed time?

_____

If so, what time did you have to be in bed by?

_____

How old were you when this bed time was enforced?

_____

_____

What was the latest you were ever allowed to stay up?

_____

What was the occasion?

_____

_____

_____

Did your parents ever employ any comfort touches to soothe you, like scratching your back, rubbing your shoulders, brushing your hair, rocking you back and forth, etc.?

_____

_____

_____

_____

Did you like to do any drawing or painting as a child?

_____

What did you draw or paint?

_____

_____

Did anyone teach you how to draw or paint?

_____

If so, whom?

_____

Did you like to do any writing as a child?

_____

What did you write?

_____

_____

Did you ever keep a diary or journal?

_____

_____

How long did you keep writing in it for?

_____

Do you still have those old journals stored somewhere?

_____

_____

_____

Did your household always have
a television?

_____

_____

If no, when did your family get their
first television?

_____

_____

Was your first television a black and
white set, or a color set?

_____

How did you adjust the antenna on
the television?

_____

_____

How did you have to change the channels on the television your family had? Did you have to move the antenna to change the channel, or was there a twist knob on the television set perhaps?

_____

_____

_____

What shows did your family watch on television?

_____

_____

_____

_____

_____

What was your favorite show to watch on television?

_____

_____

Did anyone ever make video recordings of you and your family when you were young?

_____

_____

If so, who recorded those videos?

_____

If there are video recordings Of you or your family from your younger years, do you know where those recordings are today?

_____

_____

_____

Did you ever have a Family game night?

_____

If so, what games would your family play?

_____

_____

_____

How often did you see movies at the theater, as a child?

_____

_____

How much did movie tickets cost, when you were little?

_____

_____

What was your favorite movie you ever saw in your childhood?

_____

_____

Do you remember what was the first movie you ever saw?

_____

Did you ever make a fort, or have a secret hiding spot?

_____

When did you learn how to swim?

_____

_____

Where did you go swimming as a child?

_____

_____

Did you ever go fishing or hunting, as a child?

_____

_____

Where did you fish or hunt?

_____

_____

Whom did you fish or hunt with?

_____

_____

_____

What was the biggest fish you ever caught, in your younger days ?

_____

_____

_____

Do you remember the day when you learned how to ride a bicycle?

_____

_____

How did you learn how to ride a bicycle? Did anyone help you?

_____

_____

Where did you learn to ride your bicycle to?

_____

_____

Where was the furthest away from home you ever rode your bicycle?

_____

_____

_____

Did you wear any helmet, elbow pads, or knee pads when you rode your bicycle?

_____

_____

When was your worst "wipe out" on your bicycle?

_____

_____

Did your family ever take vacations together?

_____

What was your favorite vacation that your family ever took?

_____

_____

Where was the farthest away from home that you ever traveled, before your 18th birthday?

_____

_____

Did you like to read books, as a child?

_____

_____

How often would you read?

_____

_____

_____

How often did your parents read to you?

_____

_____

_____

What was your favorite book to read, as a child

_____

_____

Did you ever play any tricks or pranks on your parents or siblings?

_____

_____

How did your parents discipline you?

_____

_____

_____

_____

_____

Did you ever have to return anything that you stole, as a child?

_____

How did that happen?

_____

_____

_____

What was the biggest thing you ever got in trouble for?

_____

_____

_____

_____

_____

_____

Did you ever run away or hide from your parents after you had done something wrong?

_____

_____

_____

Did you ever have a sibling or friend who got you into trouble, or who blamed you for something they did?

_____

_____

If so, were you still on good terms after that incident?

_____

Did you have a list Of household chores you had to accomplish every day or week If so, what were they?

_____

_____

Did your assigned chores change when new siblings were added to the family?

_____

How so?

_____

_____

_____

Did you ever help your dad or mom at their job?

_____

_____

How did you celebrate birthdays in your family?

_____

_____

_____

What was your favorite or most memorable birthday gift you ever received, as a child?

_____

_____

What was your least favorite type of birthday gift to receive, when you were little?

_____

_____

How did you celebrate Thanksgiving in your family?

_____

_____

How did you celebrate on New Year's Day in your family?

_____

_____

Were there any holidays that your family celebrated when you were growing up, which most other people don't celebrate?

_____

If so, what were they and how were they celebrated?

_____

_____

_____

How have the ways you celebrate holidays changed between the time you were a child and now?

_____

_____

_____

What is your happiest memory from childhood?

_____

_____

_____

What is your saddest memory from childhood?

_____

_____

_____

What was the angriest you ever got, as a child?

_____

_____

_____

_____

What was the worst injury you ever got, as a child?

_____

_____

How did your parents react to the injury?

_____

_____

_____

Did you ever get into a physical fight with another child?

_____

If so, what caused it and how did it turn out?

_____

_____

_____

What is the grossest thing you ever saw or experienced, in your childhood?

_____

_____

_____

Did you ever do anything that embarrassed your parents?

_____

_____

_____

Did you ever frighten your parents half to death?

_____

_____

_____

_____

Did you ever get sprayed by a skunk as a child?

_____

If so, how did it happen and how was it remedied?

_____

_____

_____

What is your scariest memory from childhood?

_____

_____

_____

_____

_____

What was the one thing you were always most scared of, as a child?

_____

_____

_____

_____

Do you remember any particularly frightening nightmares you had as a child?

_____

_____

_____

_____

_____

What are some of your most memorable dreams that you had as a child, either scary or non-scary?

_____

_____

_____

_____

_____

_____

_____

_____

_____

_____

_____

_____

_____

Do you remember the name Of the dentist you went to, as a child?

_____

_____

How did you like that dentist?

_____

_____

_____

How did you feel when you went to the dentist office?

_____

_____

_____

Did you ever get cavities In your teeth as a child?

_____

_____

_____

What did you do when you had a loose tooth as a child?

_____

_____

Did you ever knock a tooth out by injury?

_____

If so, what happened?

_____

_____

_____

Who was your family doctor, when you were a child?

_____

_____

Did they make house calls or did you go to their clinic?

_____

_____

How often did you have to go to the emergency room as a child?

_____

_____

What were the causes for having to go there?

_____

_____

_____

_____

What are some Of the biggest crimes you remember being committed in your community, when you were a child?

_____

_____

_____

_____

_____

How did your community treat the criminal who committed that crime?

_____

_____

_____

_____

_____

Did you ever have a crime committed against you or your family, when you were a child? Was your house ever robbed,or was anyone ever attacked?

_____

_____

_____

_____

_____

_____

_____

_____

_____

_____

_____

_____

What is something that you were just never able to understand,as a child?

_____

_____

What is the funniest thing you ever remember saying, as a small child?

_____

_____

_____

Did you ever do anything really foolish, as a child?

_____

_____

_____

_____

Did one of your siblings ever do anything really foolish?

_____

_____

_____

Did you ever win any trophies or awards, as a child?

_____

_____

_____

What was your proudest moment from childhood?

_____

_____

_____

_____

Which of your siblings did you look up to and want to emulate the most?

_____

_____

Why did you look up to that sibling?

_____

_____

_____

Do you think any of your younger siblings ever looked up to you and tried to emulate you?

_____

Which ones, and how so?

_____

_____

_____

_____

What is one thing you wish your parents had done, but they never did or perhaps never had a chance to do?

_____

_____

_____

What is one thing you are particularly grateful to your parents for doing?

_____

_____

_____

What was your favorite restaurant to eat out at, as a child?

_____

_____

Did your family move often, during your childhood?

_____

_____

Did you like or dislike moving?

_____

_____

Can you remember all the different places you lived, and what years or dates you moved?

_____

_____

_____

_____

_____

_____

_____

Which move was the hardest on you?

_____

_____

_____

_____

Which move were you most excited and optimistic about?

_____

_____

_____

_____

What was the first school you attended?

_____

Can you remember the names of all your grade school teachers ?

_____

_____

_____

_____

_____

_____

_____

_____

_____

_____

_____

_____

What were your favorite subjects in grade school?

_____

_____

_____

_____

What were your least favorite subjects in grade school?

_____

_____

_____

_____

Did you play any junior sports in grade school?

_____

_____

_____

What were your favorite and least favorite sports to play in grade school?

_____

_____

_____

Who was the coolest or most popular kid in your class?

_____

Why were they so cool or popular?

_____

_____

_____

_____

_____

Do you know what ever became of that person?

_____

_____

_____

_____

Did you play any musical Instruments in a band during grade school?

_____

If so, which ones?

_____

_____

_____

_____

If you were in a school band, what songs that you played in your school band do you remember the best, or which songs were your favorites to play?

_____

_____

_____

_____

_____

_____

Did any of your siblings or cousins go to school with you?

_____

_____

If you had siblings or cousins that went to school with you, what classes or school activities did you participate in with them

_____

_____

_____

_____

If you had siblings or cousins that went to school with you, did you spend a lot Of time with them?

_____

_____

What was one of your favorite class field trips that you took?

_____

_____

_____

_____

Were you ever disciplined by a teacher or sent to the principal's office?

_____

If so, what happened?

_____

_____

_____

_____

How often was your school delayed or cancelled due to snow or other inclement weather?

_____

Were you ever prevented from getting to school because of snowy roads or flooded roads?

_____

_____

If you lived In a snowy area, what kind of games and activities would you play in the snow?

_____

_____

_____

_____

If you lived in a non-snowy area, do you ever remember any rare instance where it actually snowed? Was that the first time you saw snow In real life? What did you do when it snowed?

_____

_____

_____

_____

Did you ever experience hurricanes as a child?

_____

If so, do you remember living through a particularly intense one?

_____

_____

_____

_____

Did you ever see a tornado as a child?

_____

If so, what happened?

_____

_____

_____

What would you and your family do
when the electricity in your house went
out, when you were a child?

_____

_____

_____

_____

What kind of car(s) did your family
have when you were growing up?

_____

_____

_____

_____

_____

Do you remember when your family got the car(s)?

_____

_____

_____

_____

_____

Do you remember where your family bought their car(s) from?

_____

_____

_____

How were those cars different from the cars today?

_____

_____

_____

Were you ever prone to getting motion sickness while riding in cars ?

_____

_____

Did you ever learn how to drive a car?

_____

If so, how did you learn?

_____

_____

_____

Who taught you how to drive a car?

_____

What make and model was the car you learned to drive with?

_____

_____

Printed in Great Britain
by Amazon